BEAR BONES
& FEATHERS

BEAR BONES
& FEATHERS

LOUISE · BERNICE · HALFE

COTEAU BOOKS
WWW.COTEAUBOOKS.COM

Edited by Patrick Lane.
Cover painting, "Broken Hearts, Strong Bones," acrylic on paper, 1993, by Ruth Cuthand. Courtesy of the artist.
Painting photographed by Zach Hauser.
Author photograph by Don Hall.
Cover and book design by Duncan Campbell.

Printed and bound in Canada at Imprimerie Gauvin.

Canadian Cataloguing in Publication Data

Halfe, Louise, 1953-
Bear bones & feathers
(The Wood Mountain series ; 12)

Poems.

ISBN 1-55050-055-4
I. Title. II. Series.
PS8565.A44B4 1994   C811'.54 C94-920039-5
PR 9199.3.H34B4 1994

PRINTING 07-2018

2517 Victoria Avenue
Regina, Saskatchewan
Canada   S4P 0T2
www.coteaubooks.com

Available in Canada from:
Publishers Group Canada
2440 Viking Way
Richmond, British Columbia
V6V 1N2

Coteau Books gratefully acknowledges the financial support of its publishing program by: the Saskatchewan Arts Board, The Canada Council for the Arts, the Government of Saskatchewan through Creative Saskatchewan, the City of Regina. We further acknowledge the [financial] support of the Government of Canada. Nous reconnaissons l'appui [financier] du gouvernement du Canada.

This book is dedicated
to the memory of my brother
Peter Ivan Halfe,
1950-1975,
and my daughter
Soogaymoo, 1978.

To my Grandmothers & my Grandfathers
and to those who've danced before us.

Ni tipeyihtenan ōhi acimōwina
We own these stories.
The Marrow.

contents

J

Bone Lodge

I sleep with *sihkos*.
In the fog she untangles
my braids.

I chant with robin
the shawl dance of
iskwew.

I weave with spider
the journey's *ahcāhk*.

I'm squirrel's mouth
the first time of pleasure.

I thunder *paskwāw-mostos*
in ribbons of sage.

I'm meat and bones,
dust and straw,
caterpillars and ants
hummingbird and crow.

Of these I know
in the bones of the lodge.

Ghost Dance

I shall not be there. I shall rise and pass.
Bury my heart at Wounded Knee.

They are in hills,
in bush and prairie
clattering
shattered bones
chattering
laughing the dark.

Star after star
the wind carries the knuckle of
whistling songs.

They dance
gathering quills, moss
clay, feathers and
bear bones
to flesh themselves.

The drum beats
Big Foot
dancing
whistling eagles
laughing, laughing
these shattered,
gathered bones.

Ayamihāwina – Old Rock Mother

There is no fear.
No reason to return.
I am gone
into the wilderness
of the sweat,
bleeding
Rock.

Crying for Voice

I must pull frog
pry its webbed feet
from snails in
my throat.

Kneel, fold my hands
invite weasel to untangle
my braids.

Boil duck, rabbit, fish
scoop out brain,
eyes and tongue
roll them
inside my gut.

Pull out tapeworm
chop onions, grind peppercorns
fill the intestine
with fresh blood.

Boil bible and tripe
clean off grass,
boil and boil
pebbles bubbling
soup.

Suck marrow from tiny bones
fill the place
where frog left slime
and salted snails
fell.

I'm fluttering wind
tobacco floating
against my face
mosquitoes up my nostrils
swatting memories
inside marrow.

Spirits

The veins throb
splattering
red the sky.

Comes the
night travelling
blood
swirling skirts
lifting
swishing moccasins.

Swaying bodies
in the beat of rawhide
in the beat of drum
the breathing Native lung.

Nodding heads
join swinging hands
shuffling deer-skinned feet
sweet bodies

babies
released from
the belly tie
spurt blood

Cover hay and furred bed
wolf-mother rejoices,
echoes the chant.

Red sky, night travelling
sweet bodies, four-legged ones
wolf-mother's blood
wolf-mother's voice

Dancing, dancing the union
swirling skirts
moccasin feet.
The beating common lung.

Pākahkos

Flying Skeleton
I used to wonder where
You kept yourself.
I'd hear you rattle about
Scraping your bones

I opened a door
You grinned at me
Your hollow mouth
Stared through my heart
With empty eyes.

You lifted your boney hands
To greet me and I
Ran without a tongue.

You jumped on my back
Clinging to my neck you hugged
My mound of flesh.

For a thousand years you were
The heavy bones
The companion who would not leave.

You knocked your skull
On my head
I felt your boney feet.
I dragged and dragged
I couldn't carry
Your burden more.
I pried you loose
Bone after bone.

We stood, skull to face
Pāhkahkos, your many bones
Exposed
I, lighter than I could stand.

I fed you the drink of healing
You ran skeleton fingers
Down your face and onto mine.

I gave you a prayer cloth
I wove a blanket of forgiveness
You covered us both, skeleton and flesh.

I gave you the smoke of truth
You lit your Pipe to life
You lifted it to your ghostly mouth,
To mine.

My *Pāhkahkos* companion,
My dancing Skeleton
My dancing friend.

We carry our bundles
Side by side
Bones and flesh.

Nōhkom ātayohkān 1

Nōhkom ātayohkān
a crown of sage
covers long strands of
fringed brome hair.

Ravines cut through
the soft leather
of your face.

Your mouth a
sensous pink
wintergreen,
the movement of your long
strong neck
a graceful tree.

Old one with laughing eyes
wrap me in blanket grass
fragrant with sweet pine,
the woman-musk
of your rainfed forest.
Ground my wandering feet.

I want to cup
your breast,
a starving suckling child.
I want to drink the black and
white prayer beads
your milk spills.

Nōhkom
there are no barren lands
only a searching *ayisīniw*
snared in you.

Nōhkom ātayohkān 2

Your flaming flowers
spread on my breast,
your juices sticky between
my legs, my fingers.

I've watched life
blossom and fade from
your eyes.

You've folded flies
between your lips,
welcomed the swirl of
drinking hummingbirds.
You have coated bumblebees
with sunrays.

You have left me spent
lying open, dying
beneath the sun.

You, breathless,
sightless
beneath the snow.

Sundog Mate

Pregnant for so long
Agonizing, dying
to birth.

The greased war
paint shone on the
Sun's face
Sundogs laughing
A cheering squat
All my own.

Spread my legs
Push, push,
Caught bare-assed,
again.

Damn if I'm not ready
For the challenge
The call
As I struggle.

Greasy make-up
smeared on the Sun's
Sundog face
Laugh, cheer me on
Sundog mate.

Nōhkom, Medicine Bear

A shuffling brown bear
snorting and puffing
ambles up the stairs.

In her den
covered wall to wall
herbs hang...carrot roots, yarrow,
camomile, rat-root,
and *cācāmosikan*.

To the centre of the room she waddles
sits with one leg out, the other hugged close.
She bends over her roots and leaves
sniffs, snorts and tastes them
as she sorts them into piles.

She grinds the chosen few
on a small tire grater,
dust-devils settling into mole hills.
Her large brown paws take a patch
of soft deer skin
and wraps her poultice
until hundreds of tiny bundle-chains
swing from the rafters.

The brown laboring bear
Nōhkom, the medicine woman
alone in her attic den
smoking slim cigarettes
wears the perfume of sage, sweetgrass
and earth medicine ties.

Nōhkom, the medicine bear
healer of troubled spirits.
A red kerchief on her head,
blonde-white braids hang below her breasts.
She hums her medicine songs
shuffling alone in her den where
no light penetrates, no secrets escape.

She bends and her skirt drapes
over her aged beaded moccasins.
She brushes the potions off her apron.
A long day's work complete
Nōhkom ambles down the stairs
sweeps her long skirt behind her
drapes her paws on the stair rails
leaves her dark den and its medicine powers
to work in silence.

Off with Their Heads

Nōhkom
used to take the
visiting tomcats
and ever so gently
wrap a snare wire
around their necks.

From the clothesline
we'd watch the cats
kicking, scratching,
clawing

until

they hung

limp.

Later
I'd go and examine
the stiffs.

Their lifeless eyes,
blood-filled like
late summer rosehips,
the foam around their
mouth land-salt
on a dry lake.

Flies swarmed
around the dried shit.
Ground beetles
ate their meal.

Cat stench
filled my nostrils.
I'd stumble away
clawing the invisible snare
for fresh air.

Nōhkom would sit at the window
with a cup of tea
puffing her pipe
staring at the tomcats.

Nōhkom's Ice Cream and Syrup

She'd sit on her bed
a huge broody hen
rolling long slim cigarettes
grinning through smoke-stained teeth.

"Nōhkom," I'd say, "Ice cream and syrup."
"Hāw, Kiskiman, asam picikiskisīs," she'd say.
And *Kiskiman,* my cousin, a miniature *nōhkom,*
would scuttle about, a cockroach
setting the table.

An enamel pot of woodstove tea
a roasted rabbit, head and all
legs poking out, bannock
and melted tallow: dinner is served.

"Nōhkom, ice cream and syrup."
She'd crack the rabbit head open
hand me a spoon and I'd scoop and eat
the ice cream dish.

In a chipped stone saucer
she'd pour muskeg tea
stir in *āmōmey* and
I'd slop slabs of bannock in my syrup treat.

Nōhkom would watch
clucking her pleasure.
Smoking her long, un-cut, hand-rolled cigarettes.
She'd hand me a peppermint
smooth her wrinkled apron,
with a wave she'd dismiss
Kiskiman and me.

Behind her back *Kiskiman* would pinch
determined he was *Nōhkom's* favorite
and I'd shove and punch
pleased that *Kiskiman,* again, had to wait on me.

She Told Me

She always told me
to take a willow branch
and gently whip the spirits
out of the house
calling, calling

Āstam we are leaving
āstam do not stay.

She always told me
to put the food away at night
to cover the dishes
or the spirits
would crackle and dance
whistle in our ears
and drive us mad.

I obeyed.

She always told me
never to eat the guts of
animals while I was pregnant
or the baby would be born
with a rope around the neck.

I yearned for the guts.

She always told me
that *Nōhkom*, the medicine bag
had given her three cigarettes.
That's why the lizards
walked around inside her head.

I watched the flicker of her tongue.

She always told me
never to walk over men
while I was in my moon
or they would die from my power.

I thought that was the idea.

Grandma's Apprentice

In the end she petrified me.

Her braids snakes over each breast.
A constant stream of tobacco juice ran down her chin.
She never spoke a word of English except to laugh
"fuck you" through thin closed lips.

She was Grandma's apprentice. And when Grandma died
she took over the dark long into the night
under the light of a coal oil lamp.
The smell of skunk crept under the door and woke me
her grunting and spitting in the tobacco can,
the grinding and pounding of roots never ceased
till *mihkwāskikan* sang the first song.

She told me, "Never go alone to the spring well
down by the creek
Grandma lives in that water."
Yet
she'd pour crystal cold water in the dipper and slurp
knowing all the while the water was spirit. In the end
Her fingers curled, frozen claws
her eyes black peering from under the leaves of lids.
Her mouth a sliver.
Her back gnarled as short prairie aspen
roots digging dry sand.

I offered her the spring well on her deathbed.
She looked into the deeps of the glass.
It was only she who saw the cloudy white mist
that settled into her eyes
as she parted her crackled lips and rasped,
"Kinepīk" and sighed.

Men in My Life

Nimosōm

I never knew him. He was the man with blue/green eyes. His
white/blond hair cropped close to his skin. I'd watch him standing in
the yard with a smoke in his hand quiet as the land. His beloved Sport
stood beside him, tail wagging. I remember *Nimosōm* best with his
Clyde horses, the leather in his hand, the firm gentle giddy-up. And
when he wasn't in the field plowing or strolling the woods with the .22,
he was beside *Nōhkom* serving her sweatlodge with hot rocks or lying
beside her watching through a haze of smoke. My father tells me
Nimosōm's Indian name was *Apiscāskōc,* or The Prairie Walker. I used to
think that meant He Who Took Little Steps, but it is old, pure Cree.
The Walker is a Prairie bird, just like *Nimosōm.*

I woke with the song and dance of robins, sweetgrass smells
from my father's bedroom but it was the cigarette smoke
drifting in from the outside that prompted me to step quietly
out of bed. And there on the lawn chair my father sat. He
didn't look like *Nimosōm.* My father was taller than the pine tree in my
childhood memory. He walked with the land on his back and a cane to
hold his spirit. His face was grey, his cheeks caved. His head shone in
the sun with whispers of silver, hands sun-stained. He sat quietly, facing
the sun. He told me he too was The Walker.

My husband is slouched over the soil, he lets the damp
darkness loose through thick fingers. He straightens and
brushes his face, hair tumbling around blue/green eyes, the
sun catching the horse sandy coloring of his hair. His hands
are large, firm and gentle, patient in planting seedlings.
In the woods he offers tobacco. A rifle stands beside him.
He hunts sparingly, walking the footsteps of my father's
dream, sharing the footsteps of *Nimosōm's* vision.

He Has Gone to Ground

Sometimes he wears skunk bone
or tailfeather earrings,
dyed horsehair wrapped around wire
weaved through his hair.
He bathes in sage or cedar,
sweating through breathing rocks.

When the leaves are laughing, fresh from birth,
he builds a lodge into the hill.
Like some young gopher he sweeps dirt over his shoulder,
sweat and blood running hot.

Bug-eyed spitting grasshoppers,
mink-furred caterpillars,
black ants pulling dead flies,
spiders in gunny sacks,
sparrows, hawks are his visitors.
He hears only the heart.

In sleep he sees rocks with big feet.
Old women sitting at the earth altar.
Old man smoking pipe.
A demon covered in silk,
a small woman with a whip.
He takes flight riding horses through forest,
lakes and distant lands.

Dreams, he dreams and dreams and dreams.

His lips want breast milk,
the marsh wetness of woman.
His stomach wants rubber cinnamon candies,
sweet raspberries and wild rice.
He is a mud-hen
swimming in black earth,
feet scratching his leg,
digging holes with his toes.

When the chickadees sing
he will rise,
watch the fading moon,
watch the sun-dance.
Raise his pipe and
sing the prayers of his death.
He will walk his dreams.

Rituals

The black-haired woman is tucked in her rabbit
skin blanket. Water trickles down her face.

The white-haired woman takes the grease-stained
red kerchief from her head and carefully wraps the
gartersnake skin, paper thin.
Earth smells weave around the room.
She anoints the waiting woman with
deer grease and places the crown
around the still black head.

A man with snow hair
sits puffing a cigarette
smoke haloed
green eyes pierce through eyelid slivers.

The white-haired woman turns the black head.
The razor makes little slits on her temples.
Blood sweats.
Withered lips hover
over a hollow buffalo horn and suck.
Her tongue flickers,
on a cigarette paper as she pastes peppered roots
against the moist flesh.

The black-haired woman moans while the withered
lips flap. She's a blown-out tire
on a gravel road, scolding.

Elder's Waltz

Nōhkom and *Nimosōm*
are going dancing

Tobacco offerings
ribbon cloths
Elder's murmuring
prayer songs.

Nōhkom wears pony beads
flowing flowered dress
a wide beaded belt with
hanging silver trinkets.

Campfires
muskeg tea boiling
smoke
meat drying.

Nōhkom and *Nimosōm*
are going dancing.

Nōhkom has been working for hours
on her deer-skin moccasins
soaked in tea
kneaded and stretched
dried like flannel.
Nōhkom lifts leathered legs
tugs and pulls
wraps and wraps the
hightop flaps and
rawhide thongs.

Chokecherry leather
pemmican pouch
kinnikinnick green
briar Pipe.

Her long blonde-white braids
greased with bear fat
gloss as if she's spent
hours with her porcupine brush.

Nimosōm
cropped blond-white hair
slicked down too with bear fat.
He slips on buckskin quilled jacket
over his velvet tanned leggings.
Beads and beads sparkle from
moccasin feet.

People laughing
skynight
sparkling
with fire embers.

He searches for the white-skinned drum.
His footsteps shuffle dance
to music in his head.
Tonight, tonight
the departed spirits
will feast on the bone's marrow.

Nōhkom and *Nimosōm*
are going dancing.

People squat
hands touch
circle forming.

The white-skinned drum
sends its musical tongue
colouring the air.

Blueberry, sweetgrass
offering and burning.

Nōhkom and *Nimosōm*
are dancing.

Grouse

I placed his hand on the paper,
a grouse's fantail
splayed on a dancing tree.
My drawing stick outlines
as he patiently waits.

I purr into his jackrabbit ears
and nibble his lobes.
The braided candle
flames our shadows
against the mud-straw walls.

We've few evenings like this
my father and I
when his voice drums
hunting stories.
His eyes spirit dance,
and his hands wave,
curve and buck
into creatures of the night.

Tonight I've captured them.
They rest
bark on cool leaves
and warm against my cheek.

Wagon Ride

I lean on the wagon boards
and squint over the horse's head.
Blankets of firefly snow sparkle.

Horse's nostrils
bellow clouds and form
halos around their bending heads.

Their broad bodies move
slowly through unbroken trail.

Swishing tails
they fart
as fresh horse manure
fills the air.

I look back and view
the glazing broken path
as fresh snow covers
tracks.

I peer at the skies,
stick out my tongue
catch tiny diamonds,
cross my eyes to look at
the snowflakes before they
melt on the tip of my nose.

I peep at papa.
He's dressed in his trapping beaver mitts
and fraying hudson's bay coat.
A winchester stands by his side.
His head is tilted. He's listening to
the crackling trees.
Tiny antler icicles hang from his eyelids
and underneath his nose.
His cheeks are apple red.
Still
he puffs on his hand-rolled du maurier.

Today there is no smashing fist
and kicking working boots,
no thunder of an outraged bull,
no snarling of a rabid cat.

Just me and papa
cold bound by the mute,
freezing wind.

Chokecherries

She has ghosts of blueberry shiners
and an arm glazed in strawberry stains.
Her foot is still walking sideways.
Now she stands
in front of his bed.

Her voice doesn't waver.
"*Awāsisak* they love you and look after you
I don't understand why."
She points to her foot.
She tells him, "The lizard hasn't stopped
and I still walk the dark."

He'd drink moose milk,
beat phantom lovers he caught in her arms
rocks held in the ball of his fist,
and when his fever was spent
he'd be back in the woods axing trees,
snaring rabbits or stalking deer.

She whispers, "I will stop the
tongue of lizard. Maybe
the winter squall in my chest will die."
He lies with staples in his gut,
chokecherries on his breath
and the slough in his eye.

Loving Obscenities

She always wore
those stupid
Indian Affairs glasses
that looked like
the slanted eyes of
a Siamese cat.

He always walked
stooped
puffing on Export A
disguising his whisky breath
with spearmint gum.

She always wore
a black and blue shiner
every Friday and Saturday night.
Those stupid fist marks
of his drama attacks.

His eyes moved swiftly
examining every visible track
poking and stubbing his feet
at the sign of suspected
visiting lovers.

And
When they were together
Mother and Father
He would walk ahead
muttering his loving obscenities
while she walked softly behind
staring through his head
with those cheap
Indian Affairs glasses.

Body Politics

Mama said,

Real woman
don't steal
from the sky and wear clouds
on their eyelids.

Real woman
eat rabbit well-done
not left half-raw
on their mouth.

Real woman
have lots of meat
on their bones.
They're not starving,
hobbled horses
with bony, grinding hips.

Real woman caress
with featherstone hands
not with falcon fingernails
that have never worked.

When she was finished talking
she clicked her teeth
lifted her arse
and farted
at the passing
city women.

Lizard's Curse

She came in the form of a slippery lizard
with a feather in her mouth.

She wrapped her shiny flesh
over my woman's hills and crawled my crevice.

My eyes puffed and swelled
hailstones on my face.

My head ached
heavy with rocks.

I sought the healing
mountain
and the ocean's salt.

The soft pounding
of a beating drum
and a woman's chanting song.

The sweet scent of cedar
drifted in the wind

pulling, pulling
the power of the lizard.

The skin stretched,
and my wintering flesh
hung loose against my bones.

The lizard's claws and tattered feather
left its trail of scratches in my womb.

Bled dry of tears
the ocean's coolness
flushed my wound.

The mountain cedar released healing sap
its sacred smoke smudged my temples.
The throb of darkness slipped

with the last shedding of the lizard's curse
and the woman's chant.

Free from Grandma

By the bonfire
she sits
just like grandma
with one leg tucked
the other straight out.

As she chats
she rolls
the bannock dough
on the willow stick
and props it near
the hot coals.

She pokes and strokes
one smouldering coal
and lets the ember
die beside her.

The bannock stick
turns brown and
she turns it slowly
to let the other
side bake.

With the dead
charcoal
she outlines the bottom
of her eyelids explaining
the twitching is
driving her mad
and must be cared for
because warnings are dark.

The bonfire dances
as she adds more wood
adjusting the raw meat
that hangs on the tripod.

In the hot sun
she sits
with blackened eyes
glasses perched at the
bottom of her nose

flipping through
True Romance.

She eyes
the bannock
Eyes
the fire.
Waving the smoke
hunched over like grandma.

Tuberculosis Thief

Playing
on the aspen floors by
Grandma's hearth, memories
drifted of her mama's warmth.

Listening to
the talking box
She heard her mama's voice.

She probed the nylon mesh
poked and shooked the voice box
calling Mama, Mama.
Pekīwe, pekīwe.

Hands gripped on the knobs of
the lying box,
she bowed her curly head while
the talking spirits drifted
and took her mama away.

Grandma's hand stroked her
soaking cheeks while
the child of sapling height
thought her mama dead.
The tuberculosis thief
hid in her mama's lungs
and buried her
three years
behind the sanitorium walls.

Womanchild

Your calloused burnt hands
smoothed the snarewire and formed a loop.
You said, it's so the rabbit won't get
loose and die a useless death.
Each dawn before the raven called
you nudged me awake and shooed me out the door
to see what we snared in the dark.
I walked proudly home with what we caught.
You peeled the skin, chopped off the balls
flipped them on the woodstove and fed me
the delicate taste.

Go and chop some
wood, you say.
I'll bake you
jelly rolls and cinnamon bread.
I saw and chop, toss and haul
till the wood is stacked to the cabin wall.
Tired, I lie on your bed.
Your gentle hands cover me with our crazy-quilt.
I dream of nutmeg and cinnamon cloves
and wake to the hissing of the lamp.

Dragging blankets through the woods,
you asked me not to breathe,
not to whimper, not to cry.
He's drunk again, you whispered,
as you made me a bed of spruce boughs.
There you sat while the moonlight walked
and the night hawk whistled by.

You handed me that long thick needle
with bright yellow yarn.
On the floor I crawled
behind you proudly sewing footsize stitches
on your jig-saw quilt.
I heard you crooning
what a hard-working wife I'd make.

Your swollen knees speak of crawling.
Your toothless mouth gums the Safeway rabbit.
Your arthritic hands ache to bake.
Your pleurisy mocks your laughter
beside that man wrapped inside your crazy quilt.
You the womanchild, my mother of wrinkled winters.

Ukrainian Hour

She spins from her belly
button-lint weaving,
pulls from her mouth
finger stump stories.
She knits horse hair
whipping the stick
of laughing songs.

She weaves on her knees,
humming rabbit fur stitched
between sheets of rags,
the land filled with
picket fences and tumbleweeds.

When the coal-oil lamp dances
and the cabin fire is still
Wīsahkecāhk jigs the two step
on Ukrainian Hour,
swirling her skirt,
whirling her children
in the safety of night.

Aborting

I remember
the braided wick's
tiny flame
smoking our shadows

mama lying in bed

the children
the dirt floor
making roads
and wooden squares.

mama getting up

falling

the children's
screams and screams
trying to lift mama.

the fire is out.
build the fire, she said.

That's all
I remember.

Fog Inside Mama

I'm going to take you home, Mama.

Yes, to that log shack where Papa skinned beaver
on the dirt floor.

The grass is tall. There'll be lots of mosquitoes.

Yes, Mama, the old fridge is still there and no, there's no
lightning going through to make it breathe.

The windows are broken and the barn swallows have built
their nest where the stovepipe used to smoke.

Oh Mama don't, Papa hasn't walked on that land, not for
years. Not since the last time he crushed your ribs on that
fridge.

He's on skid row somewhere.

It's safe. All we have are the old ghosts drifting
through the clouds of our heads.

Yes, Mama. I remember the tadpoles from the slough swishing
inside my red fireman's boots. They were my favorite boots.
I slept in them, I never took them off till those little
swimming snakes squished inside.

Your bones are tired and I can't find the road. I've got a
fly in my eye and it's making the rain fall from my nose.

Yes, I remember the lard pail hanging from my stomach
with a belt of twine. I'd pick so fast trying to beat Papa,
the berries drummed. Only
I never won. Papa, he picked twigs and bugs and insisted that
he had won the race.

What was that Mama?

Oh yeah, for school I had your bannock and fried rabbit.
I'd eat it *kīmōc* in the bathroom so the white kids
wouldn't laugh at me. Oh, it was good. So good.

You want some tea and a cigarette?

Yes, we're almost there.

I can see the old shack, the outhouse, the chicken coop,
the jalopy.

Yes, Mama we're going home. No more hiding.

First Moon

I
squat
in the curve of the lodge.
The air filled with muskeg and sweet blood
in dried cakes.

I cup the warmth
between my legs.
My fingers stick.
The blood ribbon
is a velvet
violent against
my flesh.

Moon rolled in my tongue,
around my fingers, and
in my bones.

I squeeze my legs,
tight.
I flow anyway, I flow.
I poke, I plug.
My finger is an infant rabbit
slaughtered out of the mother's belly.

Will my baby be a rabbit?
Wet, slippery, and red
like the silent creek between my legs?

I sit in my lodge
tangle of legs and arms.
Clumps of wet moss on the skin of earth,
mats between my legs.
The moon's child
bleeding the night.

Emma

Emma had scabs
all over
under her beehive hair
under her panties
everybody
shunned her.

She hid from the sun.
If she didn't
the hot rays would get her
scratching
until
rivers of red glistened
and
clusters of dried meat covered her.

I played with Emma.
We formed a leper colony.

Shunned
we had our moon together.
Nobody ever knew.

Emma she walked straight and proud
with that rag between her legs
I walked with a book in front of me.

Scabs and rags, Emma and me.

Bareback in the Snakehills

She went home with
cowboy legs
unable to close them.

Her grandma said some boys
had shoved
their *micakisīs*
up her
hole.

She doesn't know where
grandma got that idea.

The doctor said it was a
broken
hymen.

She didn't know that
hymns were sung between
her legs.

Just blood on rags
that ran
from bareback riding
in the hills.

Maintain the Right

Sixteen
wearing white shorts
platform shoes

He picked her up
drove
down a country road

Stopped and pushed her out.
Ordered a *blow job.*
She didn't understand.

He pushed her head
between his legs

Said a girl dressed like her
gave head
to cops like him.

Her hair held by
gripping hands
her mouth full

She gagged
with every motion.

Mud stained
she walked back to
the cruise car

and shoved her finger
down her throat.

He
watched.

Ditch Bitch

She never felt the piss of dogs
bleeding in the rain,
tongues of thistle weeds
tearing her moonlit mud skin.

She lay in this ditch
a ghost of twenty-three earths.

A woman older than the trees
of the Drumheller coulees
carrying a knapsack of roots,
pushing beer bottles
into the large folded apron
of her skirt,
singing the morning song

*Waniskā
pe wāpan ōma
āsay piyesīsak
nikamowak
miyohtākwan
kitaskīnaw.*

The song stirred the ghost
and her outstretched arm
fell on the chest of the mother.

Men plastered to her mouth,
her belly and her spoon,
stripped her skin,
fell to the wasted water of blood.

The ditch,
an open mouth of mudslides,
formed a lodge of sticks and hides.
The old woman held a horse blanket,
covered the holes of the hurting flesh.

Together they sang
drumming the song

Arise
dawn has come
already the birds sing
and the earth
delights with life.

Valentine Dialogue

I got bit.

By what?

A snake bite.

Where?

In my spoon. Gon er eeah.

Wholee sheeit.

Love he dold me.

I have a pain in my heart.

Fuckin liar.

Hate all of them.
Dink day can hang dair
balls all over da place.

Cross my legs next dime.

Mudder says day all alike.

Snake in dair mouth
snake in dair pants.
Guess dat's a forked dongue.

Mudder says I'II never lift it down.
Fadder says I'm nothin but a cheap dramp.

Shame, shame
Da pain in my heart hurts, hurts.

My brown tits
day shame me
My brown spoon
fails me.

Tired of sinning.
Dew ya dink confession will help?
Dew ya dink prayers will clean me?
Maybe I be born again.
Da pain in my heart hurts, hurts.

Durty priest
Jest wants da durty story.

Fuckin men.

Day dink I a cheap badge
to hang on dair sleeve, as if
I an easy spoon.

A dongue in dair mouth.
A dongue in dair pants.
No nothin 'bout the heart.
No nothin 'bout my soul.

Day lookit my mouth.
Must be a nice mouth
cuz I see da look
in dair eyes.

And my mouth
wants
to feel dair wet lips.

It's mudder's fault
never told me right from wrong
Fadder's fault
always say mudder a slut.
Guess I must be one too.
Guess I showed dem.

Meet nice man one day.
Maybe brown.
Maybe white.
Maybe black.
Maybe yellow.

Won't show
my body talks.
Won't tell
'bout the snake bite.

Eatin' Critters

We would stand
on the skirt of the hill
survey the stubble land
as hawk eyes marked our kill.

Ears like wings on a gliding hawk
ball cap low on his brow
lard pail and killing rock
chewing gum with me in tow.

I'd wet my finger
to test the wind.
He'd scold me if I slowed
and pinch my suntanned skin.

Tilted head and twitching ears
would listen to the gopher's pierce.
We'd spot our ground-belly meal,
race to the ditch and fill the pail
and give the hole a chug-a-lug.
When the whiskers breathe,
catch the gopher's tail.

Flatten his head with my rock
throw his dripping skin in the pail
swagger my hips like a satisfied cock
clowning home with my brother's grin.

Sugar Beat

Lethbridge
        Taber
                Raymond
                        Coaldale

Day all da same.
Busting my ass
hoeing down dem weeds
'tween sugar beets.

Eight quarters a hour
for a friggin' sun burn.
Me durns dar black.
Muskkills aches.

Drag dired body to
Chicken coop hut.

Fry Indian steak
stir a bit o'
Mac a roonie.

Count da bed bugs
crawling der way to
stinking mattress.

Itch and scratch
before I hit da pillow
Friggin' chickens
left der mess
in sugar shack.

Domorrow paycheque
Buy a beer, buy players,
catch a movie, pretend I
still a kid.
Eat bobcorn
and watch
Kemo sabe
Lone Ranger.

i bring my sins to geesuz

dear geesuz

i liked it when my mouth stayed
stucked on his
i never wanted
to take them off
years later
i feel his wetness

riding that greyhound
sitting in the back seat
his little brother asleep
i feel his hard

we played cowboys and indians
chasing each other
no one else exist
one fleeting kiss
was all i got

when my tits exploded
he ignored me
i lurked beside the girls
he fingered

one drunken night he came
and slept
six feet deep,
he buried
my dream.

Nīcimos

1960
William walked by my desk
and dropped a torn crumpled paper.
Teacher is not looking.
Hiding behind a book
I carefully reveal the scribbled
words.

William is tall with silky brown skin
his gleaming black eyes
look over at me while I hide behind my book
one eye peering out at him.

1966
I ran into Marvin on the staircase.
I mumble a shy hi and dared to look at him
as he walked up.
He looked down and stopped my flight by the
whisper of my name
and cupped my chin as he leaned over the rail
to plant a soft kiss.
For months I touched my mouth, Marvin still
hovering over me.

Marvin and I use to play cowboys and Indians.
Him in his halfbreed green eyes, mother said
he was treaty, would run after me with two guns blazing
and I the Indian would slow my running feet
so Marvin could kill me and I'd fall.

1968
I was in grade 8 when William stroked my jeans
and his hands slid over my training bra.
My body tingled and I shot out of the cabin, crimson
on my face. I never saw William again,
they say he married and became an alcoholic.

1973
Smoking grass high in the stone hills
emerald eyes and moustache smile
charmed the clothes off my skin.

1975
Sixty dollars I paid for his wedding band,
Fifty dollars he paid for mine.
The elopement in some penthouse
the dinner party at Prince Edward Hotel
of Edmonton lobster and prime Alberta steak.

Valentine's day he gave me daffodils with
two babies on my breast.

And I
in turn
gave him tangerine, plum, candy apple lips.

Thieves

Daddy lifts
his fists and
knocks it against
mommy's cheek.

Brother tells me
I can't pee standing up.

Daddy he praises me
when I chop wood
and bring rabbits home
and hoe down weeds.

***

In mission school
the nuns cut my long hair
and cover me
in thick dresses.

When I shower
they cover my tits and my bum
take a scrub brush to my back.

That boy he corners me
and touches
my spoon and makes
me cry.

In church on my knees
I pray to father
about that dirty hole.

In the classroom
when I talk
when I write about the boosh
they laugh and scold me
make me stand in the corner.

And that girl
with thick lips
mean talk
her stick
scares me.

And that nun
in black robes
with prayer beads
makes me peel potatoes
makes me iron sheets
makes me polish the floors
and strips my lumpy bed.

***

I feel good with beer
drink the boys
wear make-up
and sexy clothes
show off my legs.

I travel to Jamaica
go to university
and laugh at that old
broken English.

I've dumped religion
and sit cross-legged in the
sweatlodge, chanting songs.

I've married   *well.*

Boarding School

In the late fall
ice waited
outside our cabin.

Inside
crackling fire
licked the guts
of the woodstove.
The coal oil lamp
flickered in the
one-room shack.

Two white-skins
talked in tongues.
Father's long face
stretched further
to the floor.
Mother's crimson cheeks
turned like swirling ashes
in the stove-pipe.

Behind
Mother's draping dress
a six-year-old sister.
Her small fist
white against
brown skin.

I sat behind a
thick home-made
wooden table,
trembling.
My stomach couldn't hold
the fresh cinnamon roll.

The air was
wrapped in
raven darkness.

Namōya māskoc.
It's a mistake.
Father's voice
shook.
Mother swayed.

The white-skins
left.
The cold seeped in the
cracks of the door,
its fingers wrapped
in silence.

The world
was silent.

The family gone.

The family not ever more.

The Residential School Bus

A yellow caterpillar,
it swallows them up.

The little brown ones their stained
faces in the windows   skinny and thick
black braids   pressing hands
grease the glass.

On its back the caterpillar
carries hand-sewn canvas bags.

Outside against the evening sun
the mothers, the fathers,
shrink.

They cannot look
at the
yellow caterpillar.

***

The building is huge
with long white empty hallways.

A child walks softly
the echo runs ahead of her.

The smell of Lysol
and floor wax
overwhelms the memory of wood smoke
and dirt floors.

***

At night the little ones
press their bodies
between cold starched sheets.
Somewhere
someone
in the huge dorm
sobs quietly.

The child
clenches
two purple
suckers
underneath her pillow.

She won't eat them,
not for a
while.

***

They line up for breakfast
and receive wonderful bowls of porridge.

She loves porridge.
Her mama always made her porridge.

She looks up and sees
her favourite brother.

Ivan's ears look like
two gliding hawks.
They've given him a crew cut.

Charlie the eldest brother
is in the big boy's room.
She doesn't see him
and doesn't care.

Her eyes linger on
Ivan. They smile.

She swallows
the porridge
that is stuck in her
throat.

***

Geesuz
is always mad.

She sits too often
in the confessional.
She kneels too often
in front of geesuz.

***

The vision box
collects people
and makes them dance.

She turns the buttons
and the dancing people
turn into black and white lines.

She kneels
in the corner.

The girl
with the mean stick
and fat mouth
hovers near her.
She's a
huge night moth
beating her wings
against the dance.

***

They've arrived.
Wagonloads of
mothers, of fathers.

The children have been
berry picking.

Sister Treebow
is like that girl
with the big lips.

Sister's lips stick out
further. The arrival of
mothers, of fathers
makes her madder.

The children
stand around the corner
of the building
wondering whose
mother, whose father
was there.

She didn't want to hope.

Father Brown
in his long black dress
calls out names.

Times are scheduled.

In the bare parlor
they sit,
mother, father, Ivan
and her big brother.

Their stiff hugs,
she wants more
but can't.

The stiffness stays.

The glass between the parlour
and the hallway is marked
with grease-stained hands
and smudges of
rain.

***

The yellow school bus
waits.

Ships on the Reserve

I grew up in mud
my dolls earth
scratchings
on lye painted walls
straw, horsehair,
a bluebird's nest
plastered by my fingers
between wind whistling
aspen cracks and
mother's quilts.

I never saw a TV
never heard of ships
yet
ships were in the
bowels of the earth
where I dug tunnels
and ate earth crumbles
devilled with tiny red
and white eggs
I'd stuff till my
tongue thickened
in blackness.

I'd emerge
slap bannock dough
on slabs of cardboard
charcoal stick figures
with long eyelashes
massive hearts
smiles stretched
across the slough
where string snakes sang.

My ship moved and
I travelled in brick walls
starched, clean as Mary
in her bluebird robe,
heart throbbing
plastered against her
chest. I pried it loose
saw through the smile.

My ship, my ship
mud   bricks
crumbling in my mouth.

Nitotem

He was tired of having his ears pulled,
squeezed and slapped
by Sister Superior. They bled and
swelled, scabbed and scaled like the brick wall.
Often he didn't hear the Sister shouting
and clapping her orders at him
or the rest of the little boys.
The others, when they could,
would nudge him so he could lip-read Sister's words.

He was embarrassed to undress in front of all the boys
and especially Sister.
At home he always looked out the window
when someone was undressing. Here everyone looked
and laughed at your private parts.
Soon they too were no longer private.

He suffered in silence
in the dark. A hand muffled his mouth
while the other snaked his wiener. He had no
other name, knew no other word. Soon it was no
longer just the hand but the push, just a gentle
push at first, pushing, pushing. Inside the
blanket he sweated and felt the wings
of pleasure, inside his chest the breath burst
pain, pleasure, shame. Shame.

***

On the reserve he had already raped two
women, the numbers didn't matter.
Sister Superior was being punished. It was
Father who said it was woman's fault
and that he would go to hell.

He walked, shoulders slightly stooped
and never looked directly at anyone.
When spoken to he mumbled into his chest.
His black hair covered his eyes. He no longer
tried to lip-read, no longer studied the
brick wall.

Bruises Are Part of Daddy's Job

His arms lie
heavy across my stomach.
He snores, dreams of
frozen fish.

The telephone rings and rings
his arm flails in the dark.

He snores
nightmares of
battered woman, death rattles,
bar fights.

He slams the phantom phone.

The hospital gown flaps
he's a pelican in the emergency room
feet stuffed in two
different shoes.

My son crawls into the grooved
folds of crumpled sheets. His face
a trail of sleep, and shadows on
his lips. I rock him, whisper

Bruises are part of daddy's job
gassing, mending, patching. Shhh.

Tribal Warfare

She pressed her tits
hard into his mouth, against his chest
held his balls in her fist.

He was so drunk he couldn't get it up.
He had promised her a good one,
damn good.

She was so horny she
cried between his legs.

Later
in the psychiatric ward
the doctor asked why
she took so many pills.

She couldn't tell him
how she wanted it so bad, it shamed her.
She couldn't tell him
the foreigner slept many nights
spent, while she wept
for *Nehiyawak.*

Hoop Dancer

She was told take a mirror and
look at your spoon when
she talked about
how

she square-danced
in a half-breed dress,
white husband in her arms.

How

She sat in the bleachers
wrapped in a blanket
wind blowing feathers
humming powwow songs.

How

She watched her husband blow
the eagle whistle
his shoulders, his knees
bobbing
blue eyes fixed on the
Sundance Tree.

How

She whistled, and hooted
stamping her feet
betting nickels and quarters
at the rodeo grounds.

And how

She's on the cruise ship
wearing a four hundred dollar
gown, lips painted red
staining the sky.

She talked
softly of being
crushed through to the bone
and willed the heart to pound.

Tonight when the music stops,
and her son's footsteps sleep
she will close the bathroom door
press the mirror between her legs
as pipe tobacco fills
her space of song.

Stones

Men
day hang dere balls
all over da place.

what I didn't no
is day
whack dem
fundle dem
squeeze dem
dalk to dem
whisper to dem
scream at dem
beg dem
pray to dem
g ah sh
even
swear at dem.

I no dese
cuz I followed dem
at dat place
where day use ghost berries
nd buff alow sticks
nd play in da
buff a low mud
nd day use dat
stick
nd whack dem
berries
into
dem
gopher holes

dere all ways drying
to put dem
dere balls everywhere
why
I evin saw dem
at dem dere
dinner dables
coloured balls
wit a big long broom
boking,
rolling,
nd smacking dem
all together
into
six holes
in dat dable.

g ah sh
wit all dat whacking
day shoold of come
a long dime ago
nd be satisfied.

but no
dere still
jiggling dem
between dere legs
drying to find
different hole
to put dem in.

dem balls by now
should be so heavee
day make dere walk
hard
liddle bit
like dem
African elephants
I saw on
DV

Hamilton's Graveyard

A seed was planted in the North Bay rain, cries, sweet cries
of night birds nesting in sheets of damp leaves.

The seed grew and swelled in the buried bodies of
my guts.

I wanted refund for my ten dollar IUD. Slanted
my eyes at the touch of the physician's hand. Swore
at the man whose pleasure I carried.

At home I thought of my mother's bitter root that would shred
my growing womb. I heard the voice of the sweetgrass braids.
I thought of another baby twisted like a knotted tree, her head
an empty bowl. My hand rested on my swollen belly.

It started with liver sliding into the toilet. Later IV
vodka to still the belt around my waist. Then an incision
traced the equator across my skin and delivered
her into my frozen arms.

She died with a head of wet dark hair shining in the butter
dish. The rain fell down my drying breasts.

Gifts for the Child

He thought of
spawning fish,
chickadees and ravens
soaring the sky
when he came inside her.

She thought of
darning socks, knitting and quilting,
pounding chokecherries, rendering fat
for pemmican winter feasts
while the aspen juice ran.

The child arrived squealing
between her legs,
an infant rabbit in elder's skin,
chokecherry stain on her back.
He smeared brain of chickadee
on the roof of the child's mouth and
she fed her marrow fat.

Rainbow Babies

They travelled west across the prairies
to visit the site of a sixty-seven
year old burial. Infant bones that
long left their song beyond the trees.
They live two hours away from
my daughter's grave. A place where dozens
of babies keep their wings warm, rubbing
bones together, dancing fireflies over
the lake, lighting candles in plastic
bouquets.

My husband and I offer saskatoons, deer
meat and wild rice to the one who
breathes the wind, the one joined
in laughter with her burial companions.
The one whose fingers I did not reach. I
will carry a bouquet of wheat, string their
heads in song. Leave it for the old bones,
the living bones, and for the wind.

Snake

I am a snake.

Comfortable in my skin.
Too comfortable. Became fat.
Cannot see. Peering
from under these hooded eyes.
Cannot hear. Skin has grown
over my ears. Cannot smell to test the air.
Thought this staleness was normal.

I am a snake.

Cheeks puffed.
Thought I could see everywhere.
Didn't realize I hadn't scaled the wall.
Didn't realize my belly was all I scratched.
Sleeping inside my skin.

I am a snake.

I begin to crack.
Shed the old. Slowly peel.
My new head emerges.
Tongue tastes the wind. Caution fills my
every bone. Raw my skin is.

I am a snake.

Vulnerable above and below. Hot rock,
cold rock. Slithering off, slithering in, slithering
down, up, around, away.

I am a snake.

Equivocating tongue.
I see the light. I see the dark.

Hold Me Tight

I went inside his belly.
I found magpies feeding on maggots,
berries rotting and whiteflies dancing.

I found a ball of hair,
a needle, a string worm
wrapped around his guts.

I sucked through the horn
and filled my mouth
with   pus.

Inside his belly
I heard the winds belch.
Chanting that
eating his heart
was the curse of his eye.

Picking Leftovers

There's men in the cellar shovelling, sweeping with combs and tooth-brushes, probing dental picks, doctors in surgical gloves cradling bones, jaws, teeth, skulls, brittle arms and legs. Glueing pieces through lenses thicker than god's eye, given birth dates and pencilled in bibles.

When I was a child, father would stop at sites we called picking left-overs. I've returned with pitchfork in my hand, hammer against my heart. I've offered tobacco to earth and raked layers of toilet bowls, tin cans, beer bottles, and open-mouthed refrigerators. The skin of earth peels leaking pails, stench buried in ceremony. And over there in marble fields boxes of bones cemented in white rock. I give them birth dates, carefully record locations and fax the findings to the ship docked, wait-ing for hundreds of years, on the eastern shore.

Diaper Boy

I was a kid my diapers full,
my legs chapped, lying against the slop pail.
They found me mosquito-bitten, snot all over
my face, flies dancing free.

I was a naked starving mouse.

I was alone in the log shack,
my mother and father at the
beer parlour. Somebody walked by and heard
my cry.

***

See my long black, black braids?
I grease them with bear fat and gloss them.
Put on my stetson
Tie a red bandana around my neck
charm the woman with beer and cigarettes
and fill them with babies.

I make women hold me.

They can't resist
my hard dark body.
I move like a mounting deer.
They caress and stroke the same arms that froze
beside that slop pail.
They kiss the snot off my face where the flies
no longer dance.

***

My ears only hear the soft warm panting.

Jahnnie

Jahnnie used to stand on the gravel
at the edge of the reserve
his arm extended, thumb pointing up
a burlap sack slung over his shoulder.

Eight o'clock in the morning
driving by in my jalopy,
still rubbing the sleep from my eyes
the radio rooster blasting the air.
I'd stop, pick Jahnnie up.

He'd open the rusty hinged door
crawl in with a smile and ask,
"Huz's da g-earls?"
Stale cigarette smoke and home-brewed beer
would sting my eyes.

His Brylcreamed hair smelled of greasy neckbones
his face oily from mouth to cheek.
He'd fumble in his burlap sack
clanking cans and spilling aged beer
from ditch-gathered bottles.

"Ciganet?" he'd ask.

Each summer each day I'd pick Jahnnie up
his dirty blue jeans
the silver of his hair
stoop of his back.
The yellow stain of his beer
sank in the sofa of my jalopy seat.

His toothless old mouth
caved-in cheeks
sagging shallow pools
beneath his eyes,
dragging his burlap sack
smoking his "ciganet"
I'd watch him straggle
his beloved gravel road
a spiritless coyote.

Lonesome Charlie,
whisky and beer
"ciganets and da g-earls"
had their ride in my Pontiac
and Jahnnie's skeleton's back.

Idylwyld Crow

Rushing home
into the dark
I drive by
a moving scarecrow.

Red cap
perched on
grey corn-husk hair
toothless mouth
jutting jaw.

Can't help but stop
and offer her a ride.
In broken English
she tells me she lives in
Kilburn.

Pulls out her blue
hospital card with
her address
explaining all the while

She's been out
buying the cheapest
stale bread in town
somewhere on Idylwyld.

A Saulteaux,
a dark crow,
feeding her children
crumbs in the city light.

Sister

In the morgue *e-pimisik,*
on a steel table.

Scarred face
crushed.
Work boots
trampled her in.

Her arm crooked
limp by her side
vagina raw, bleeding
stuffed with a beer bottle.

Pasikōk, pasikōk
Pehtāw, pehtāw
Kisimsinow pikiskwew

Akosiwak ayisiyiniwāk
Piko matotsānihk ta pimātisīyahk
Kīpa kīwek

Race with your spirits
Kākīsimotāk, to heal, to heal.

Iskwew atoskewin kimiyikonaw.
Kakweyāhok, kakweyāhok.

Pasikōk, pasikōk
Pehtāw, pehtāw
Kisimsinow pikiskyew.

Akosiwak ayisiyiniwāk
Piko matotsānihk ta pimātisīyahk
Kīpa kīwek.
Race with your spirits
Tā kākīsimoyāhk, to heal, to heal
Iskwew atoskewin kimiyikonaw
Kakweyāhok, kakweyāhok
Ahaw.

Beneath the Eyelids

She crossed the barrier of the mind
just before sleep slid over the eyelids
and *Pāhkahkos* flooded the thin skin.

Blood ran down the skull face,
strands of black hair in patches.
Her jaw hung loose, crooked to one side.

She wailed.
The cry spun
beneath the armpit of the trees,

floated like thick smoke
to sit on the mountain tops.
Her weight was heavy on the backs of the people.

They scrambled below her, trying
to pray, to sing.
Still the bombs fell and the black grease spread.

Pāhkahkos, with her emptiness, sits
heavy with death
waning slowly as each moon
slips
beneath her eyelids.

Eclipse

As the earth travelled
between the sun
and the moon
I was a dog tearing flesh
inside my skin.
I paced the hall
swinging my head,
the rabid blood
flooding my eyes.
The moon slipped
through the sheet of dark.
I too waned
and the rainberry
words sprung from my
fingers.

So Sorry

the pope said i'm sorry
i sent a useless sack of scalped
potatoes.

he said indian agents would
give daddy a roll of twine,
a box of shells and whisky.
the spirits crawled inside
my daddy and never left.

he sent blankets
and my babies died.
he sent wooden sticks
with a dead man to hang
around my neck.

he said if i prayed
to you, geezus,
ate your body, drank
your blood,
threw out my bannock,
lived on my knees
counting stones,

i'd never be without
my family.

I'm So Sorry

I'm so sorry, the pope said
I thought you were just gathering
to lift your legs, thump your chest
around that tree of old men.
I didn't know the rock and twig
you smoked.
Blueberries, and sweetgrass
were your offerings.
I wouldn't have taken your babies
and fed them wafers and wine.

I'm so sorry, I just thought
we could borrow land for a little
to plant our seeds,
raise sheep and build churches, schools.
I really didn't know how you survived
for centuries on buffalo and teepees,
praying in medicine wheels.

I'm so sorry, I should have told
the settlers to quit their scalping,
selling hair at two bits for each Indian
I'm so sorry. I'm so sorry.
Maybe I could build healing churches
chapels full of sweetgrass and drums
chase the spirits out and fill sweatlodges
full of armed angels.

ten hail mary's

the pope said too bad that
man of sea, kelp, rancid pig
and starving teeth
came on your land.

i'm awfully sorry he ate so
much buffalo meat
gave you beads and trinkets
for beaver, coyote and mink.

he didn't mean to sleep with
your women, make them cry
and send your children to
purgatory and england too.

i'm sorry the pope said.
i'll write to the priest, the nuns,
make them say, i'm sorry too
for *suffering little children
coming to me* in the red brick
schools.

i'll tell other people too
i'm sorry and i promise to
fold my hands and keep you
in my prayers.

In Da Name of Da Fadder

In da name of da fadder, poop
on my knees I pray to geezuz
cuz I got mad at my husband for
humpin' and makin too many babies
I 'pologize cuz I mad and cried I
didn't have no bannock and lard
to feed dem cuz my husband
drank all da *sōniyās* for wine.

In da name of da fadder, poop
my husband slap, fist and kick me
I hit him back. I 'pologize poop
da priest said I must of done someding
wrong and I deserve it cuz woman is
'uppose to listen to man. I not a good
wife cuz my hands somedimes
want to kill him.

In da name of da fadder, poop
I lookit other man he is so
handsome my eyes hurt, he kind, gentle,
soft laugh and my body wants to
feel his hot face. I no geezuz
would be mad he said I must not
be durty in my doughts but
poop I want smile and warm arms.

In da name of da fadder, poop
Inside the sweatlodge I shame cuz
Indian *iskwew* don't no anydin',
In church priest said all us pagans
will go to hell. I don't no what da means,
all I no I is big sinner
and maybe I won't see geezuz when I die.

In da name of da fadder, poop
I dought da geezuz kind but
I is no good. I can't read hen write.
I don't understand how come *mōnīyās* has
clean howse and lottsa feed and he don't
share it with me and my children.
I don't understand why geezuz say I be
poor, stay on welfare cuz *mōnīyās* say
I good for nuddin' cuz I don't have
wisdom. Forgive me poop I is
big sinner.

Der Poop

der poop
forgive me for writing on dis newspaper
i found it in da outhouse, saw lines
dat said you is sorry
some of my indian friends say is good but
some of dem say you sorry don't walk
so i was sitting here dinking dat we
maybe dalk
say, i always want to dell you stay
out of my pissness
if me wants to dalk to trees
and build nests in house
dats hup to me
if me wants to pitch my dent
and feed da ghost bannock hen berries
and maybe drow some indian popcorn
for you geezuz dats hup to me
i don't hask forgiveness not want
hand mary's, or a step ladder to heaven
me is happy with da sky, da bird *Iyiniwak,*
four-legged *Iyiniwak,* i is happy
sorry mean dat i don't need yous church
and yous priest telling me what to do
sorry mean dat i free to dalk to *Manitou*
the spirits and plant *Iyiniwak.*
dats all for now, poop
maybe we dalk again next time i see you
in da newspaper.

My Ledders

dear pope
i no, i no, you dired of my ledders
i couldn't let dis one go
i dought you could do somedin 'bout it.
years ago you stopped *nōhkom* and *nimosōm*
from prayin in da sweatlodge and sundance,
drummin, singin and dancin.
you even stopped dem from Indian speakin
and storydellin.
well you must had some kind of bower
cuz da govment sure listen.

well, pope
last night on DV
i watched some whitemen
sweat in da lodge, and at
dinner dime on da radio
i heard dat man dell us
dat some darafist was havin a retreat
and to register.
what dat mean, i not sure.
anyway he is buildin' a sweatlodge.
i never hear anybody before on da radio
dell da whole world dat.
i sure suprise and kinda make me mad.

i wonder if you could dell da govment
to make dem laws dat stop dat
whiteman from dakin our *isistāwina*
cuz i dell you pope
i don't dink you like it
if i dook you
gold cup and wine
pass it 'round our circles
cuz i don't have you drainin
from doze schools.
i haven't married you jeesuz
and i don't kneel to him,
cuz he ain't my god.

dese men, pope, don't know what
tobacco mean, what suffer mean,
alls dey no is you jeesuz die for dem
dey don't no what fastin' mean
dey jist dake and gobble our *mātotsān*
as if dey own it.
dey don't no what it mean to dake
from da earth and give somedin' back
i so dired of all dis *kimoti,* pope
deach your children.
eat your jeezuz body.
drink his blood.
dell dem to go back to dere own deachings,
pope.

Returning

It's raining, and the salt slides down my face into my mouth. Blue Quills Residential School, the log cabin. Memories. I summon them all.

I have been asked many times, wasn't residential school better than the fires that raged at home? I don't find that a fair question. My grasshopper legs clung only to the crippled love I came to know. It lay for years snared within the red walls of the residential school. Such shame. Such assault. That's what it was, refined under the rule of reading, writing, and arithmetic, and a god that had the eyes of a roving fly. This god wore black robes, cowls, and beads. Pebble beads, hard and polished as wind-swept rocks with silver and wood crosses where jesus died for my sins.

I grew up behind those walls. Six years. I knelt each morning in the chapel, up at dawn to pray to jesus to save my soul. I hoped that I would win an award for being the most pious, most committed at the end of the year. I can't help it when the buds between my legs tingle. I can't help it when my eyes stray to explore the tits of other girls. Why must I hide my body, jesus? The rags that I wear when I shower are so heavy, will I ever be clean? The scrub brush is not hard enough.

And jesus, can you tell me how to love a boy? I must not have such dirty thoughts or I will get purgatory and venial sin. I can't tell the priest in the confessional, so I write my sins and ask for penance.

At night I leave tears. I want my mother, my father, my brothers, my sister. I hold a sucker from my brother underneath my pillow. For weeks I take only a lick. I peek at my brothers across the dining room. I mustn't look too long. Why can't I look and talk to my brothers? At home during the laughing bloom of leaves we fight and cheat at our games. They call me ugly and flat chested. I hate them. In them I see my father, double tongues of laughter spinning my thoughts. Yet we work together and marvel at the wood stacked for our parents. We want to surprise them, but they never say a word. They too are the children of residential school. We know only how to show anger. We are always suspicious of one another. Watching, forever watching.

The little girls hate me. There is one with big lips assigned to the ruler. I hate her. She slaps us hard. We stand around the girl with white skin when its her turn to have her hair combed. One, two, three, ah, the numbers are too great. Lice. We are in awe, yet we shame her as she wins the count. At home my mother creams my hair with kerosene and I sit till all the bugs are dead. With gentle hands she pulls white nits. I listen to her murmur stories of *Wīsahkecāhk*. Her hands are two dead branches at her side when I leave for residential school. I see her next, when the pussy willows green. Her eyes will be bruised and black.

Father hands me the butcher knife and tells me to take over the skinning of the deer, but first he salts the fresh kidneys he's brought home. He never tells me, but I hear him brag that I'm a good little skinner. I never know when the thunder will burst, never know when the lightning will strike. My memories roll inside my stomach. Mean little butterflies at home, and at residential school.

The supervisor has huge keys hanging from her skirt. Everywhere we go she pulls her keys to unlock the stores of toilet paper, towels, Sunday morning tams. We are given three sheets of toilet paper. We learn to fold and refold. A hundred little squares of shit squeezed inside my heart. I didn't know I had locked away these memories, the keys jingling in the corridor of other people's stories.

I remember my first kiss. I received it on the staircase, treasured the feel of my first love's mouth for months. I didn't know what to do with him. Love was saliva, tongues of tobacco smoke, the hidden spirits.

Yet, when the life in my belly kicked and milk trickled down my breasts the mountains called. The sweet sweetgrass smoke and the sweatlodge rocks woke my spirit. I knew then where I was cradled.

You've Got to Teach White Women Everything

I've tasted myself.
Gooseberries, pin cherries and
rosehips rolled between my teeth,
stretched till my bones bent
and my breath was wind.

I've tasted the tongue of
bear, deer and dog,
left camomile in the corners of my
mouth.

I've tasted
the sweet drip of sea
drying between my thighs
belly sweat breathing
on my breast.

I've tasted chocolate raisins
on my spine, rolling raspberries
between my toes and the breath
of swallows, feathers on my face.

I've tasted
till I'm swollen with sleep.

These are the Body's Gifts

I offer ribs, taut flesh stretched like a starving dog's. My
tits scratching sidewalks.

I offer belly, wedged in spandex. A pit of balled snakes
quivering beneath touch.

I offer buttocks, rump of deer sailing over fences.
Wēpāyōs: white tail flipping.

I offer thighs, the smoke of a .303, fingers unclenched.

Take this body of snails and leeches. Stretched babies that
have left dried creek beds across the gut.

Take it, take it, pressed tight in your beak.
Beady eyes examining its old, tender flaws.
Marvel at the rot.

Inside you, Magpie, I will be the glutton eating flesh,
curing the dysentery of age.

for Usine

A pigeon gathers pebbles on the freeway
sidestepping the traffic.
A ladybug walks on the edge of a large envelope
on my husband's desk.
The death of a tree goes unnoticed,
a deep white glare rooted to the earth.
My son's girlfriend leaves robot kisses on the telephone.

I've squirted my baby boy in the eyes
with my left breast, suckled him with both.
His teeth chewed the teats like rubber.

The black fur of a flattened dog outlined
on the pavement.
There is no game, no fur, no berries
just bones and chains at Mendel Art Gallery.
Laughter of nursery children under the glass
teepee at *Wanuskewin.*

My teats are kneaded buckskin, his baby fingers
grooved into the smooth folds of skin.
We saved his penis from the slicing knife.

At thirteen my sister wiped the smells,
filling my diaper with fresh moss.
She stopped my wails with her large toe
unable to find the soother filled with cow milk.

In grade one he clung, screaming. My stretched breast
empty. He slept with a wooden sword. At dawn he laughed
at a battle he'd won with a skeleton of clothes.

We were hungry. My brother and I squeezed the
infant rabbits from twisted guts. Dug small
potatoes, wild onions and made a broth. Wrapped
bannock dough on willow. Sugarbeet parents never knew.

He was standing on a float with a chainsaw larger than
the baby skunk he cradled for comfort. Threw candies at his
sister and me. I grinned, yelled through the crowd, I love
you, my baby. Years later I learned how the snare of pride
and shame strung him.

The wind tears leaves off sleeping trees. The magpies
are cocky. Soon they'll be black specks against frozen
white. I hope I can keep the car on the road. My hands are
my eyes guiding the steering wheel over black matted fur. My
hands caress the curves of my breast and hibernate with the
ladybug, hopscotch between hundreds of rolling
tires, send puckered kisses to bald-headed babies. They are
bark of dead trees. My hands limp while my baby answers
Janice's call, puckering the air.

I dream a ghost speaking through my body. Three nights of
dreaming. I drink four cups of coffee, my eye bags reaching
the brim. I don't sleep till I hear his footsteps above
my bed.

His first girlfriend was a short fat kid. She was twelve
with long tousled hair. She acted like a starved-loved cat,
rubbing up and down his leg.

My cousin said she was three when the dirty old man first
touched her. Her memories are dead inside her, when the
little snake crawls between her legs they are alive. I
remember peeing in the dark outside the beer parlour,
that dirty old man was suppose to keep an eye out. I ran and
ran with my panties down.

Me, I'll keep my snot, fold my squares of Kleenex.

I hope he wears rubbers.

for Omeasoo

I lift my wrist
suck out marrow
blow into my daughter.
I spoon the spill
into her lips.

I lift my mother's finger,
add *Nōhkom's* ashes,
and stir.

My daughter dances
a leaf twirling
on the wind.

She blows the baritone
a gosling calling,
Kīwētinohk.
She delivers
dried meat and croissants
to *Nōhkomāk.*

She is a rainbow,
the give-away feast
of our blood.
She bleeds.

for Patrick

I held him on the hill
water on his face
the bruised scales glistened on his back
beneath the full moon.
He cupped his hands
offered his soul. I took,
filled his body with trees;
he hacked and sawed for spare change.
Filled his body with women and children;
he danced them with whisky and longings
of the hills, turned and walked his road,
kicking gravel in his way.
Always his pipe tobacco lingered.

I filled his eyes with cheating men
rolling in fat thighs,
gambling cowboys on the tracks.
A magpie stealing guts in skidrow
vomiting them in his maggot nest.
Silver coins in his eyes,
Window Pane on his tongue,
soaring through glass and shrapnel,
his childhood left
on the hill of his back.

I filled his mouth with skunk juice,
rat root and honey. I clipped his wings, one flew
to an Indian woman who wove it into blankets.
His teeth sit on a pelt by his bed.
His memories blood skies, his father's bullet,
the leather whip of his hand,
his beak attacking stories of the heart.
From the earth he draws my breath,
music of frogs, crickets, cats and dogs,
wolves and bears.
And a woman.
Always the tobacco lingers.

Landscape

I have set his feet on soft ground:
I have set his feet on the sloping shoulders of the world.

I've walked the land till ravines swallowed my feet.

Tobacco was offered to fire and earth
the fire came out to lick the dead grass. That spring
the cabin burned where I had filled my life with laughter
and anger. Only the cellar is left.

A young girl, a two-year-old boy cry with coyotes,
their mother's bones mending in the hospital,
their father selling horses and cattle for wine.
I see them running along the creek, two young coyotes
yelping. I take the .22 and fire into the air.

Many winters have passed and the coyotes have grown straggly
with hunger, their eyes shrivelled rosehips.
Their yelping has turned into moans. Years ago
Wīhtikōw reached inside their guts, where its roots grew
into their hair, into their fingers and feet, their hearts
frozen. Coyote pups now roam that creek, sniffing
for their parents. They run side by side, hungry.

I dreamt I was filling the cracks of the cabin
with paper and books while the wind told stories. An old
bear lit the coal oil lamp. In her hand she held sweetgrass.
Later climbing a hill I found four feathers, and
three coyotes following.

I've become arched feet inside my shoes. I will find those
.22 bullets and hit the mark.

The Way to the Heart

Wīhtikōw travels
with a hatchet, bladder pail
and snares.
His ragged moccasin feet bare
to thistles, to rocks, to snow.

He boils robins and sparrows.
The tiny bones stain
necklaces, little skulls on breasts.
He lives a lonely life
filled with relatives in his gut,
dreaming of fat Indians
in the deep of winter.

Wīhtikōw and *Wīsahkecāhk* meet.
Wīsahkecāhk is a laughing fox,
coyote, and word-hustler.
Chickadee sings about the time *Wīsahkecāhk*
ate dry meat-scabs that fell off his rump.

Wīhtikōw casts a spell.
He thinks.

Wīsahkecāhk dances,
building fires for *Wīhtikōw*. Dancing the feast of death.
Sihkos, slender weasel, little brother
pokes his breath
to watch the dance and feast of bones.
Dance, oh dance, little brother,
travel the back hole of
Wīhtikōw. Cut the straps
inside his chest. Tomorrow
you will be most celebrated.

And when *Wīhtikōw* blew
the fire rose, the back hole
opened, foul wind breathed.
Little brother travelled
up the dark passage
to the North
and the heart of *Wīhtikōw* was cut.

Wīsahkecāhk, spirit of vision
Wīhtikōw, spirit of twisted hunger,
they dance, they dance,
come alive, come alive. Let
tobacco speak, the spirit
of *sihkos* will free you.

The Heat of My Grandmothers

The old man calls my *Nōhkomāk*
a bunch of bitches, *pisikwātisiw.*

Yes, I took painted warriors:
molded their sinew thighs,
into my flesh.
Our spirits moaned, laughing between
teepee poles reaching the heavens,
stars leaping against the breathing hide.

I was fourteen winters when I was told
my first husband was the elder's choice.
That winter in our teepee
the smoke couldn't hide
the fragrance
of muskeg tea
and juniper
we mixed between our bodies.
The second winter two calves
dropped to the earth.

My first husband's bones
I found beneath the autumn buffalo,
his arrows in the meat. My moccasins heavy,
I swayed the roundness of my body
wailed till the buffalo sweat
melted his skin into
the prairie grass.

My second husband of three winters
I received at a give-away between
the Blackfoot and Cree. He kissed
the valleys of my buttocks, licked
the paths of my swollen breast. He,
antelope of clouds. I,
wider than his open mouth.

I found him after a skirmish with
the white meat, a bullet between his eyes.
I was winter in my spring. My braids
greyer than the passing snow. I called
magpie, crow, and raven to clean
his body cradled in the trees.

My third husband took my calves and
gave them to the black robes. His
eyes bluer than mountain rivers, hands
took half the hide I made for travois. He'd
flicker his eyelashes; Monarchs in my sleep,
while I dreamt of babies hungry and
frightened behind cold fences.

Ten babies. Six of prairie blood, four
of meeting rivers. A beaded rainbow,
each child suckled by my wind-bitten nipples
their fathers loved.

Roots and Wings

In the brief exchange
both dog and woman
knew he was willed
beneath the fender and the wheels.
Their eyes
met before he left.

He wasn't the first dog
to go.
Her mind twisted their guts
hands laying their skulls
under saplings.
There will be no dogs
in the city.

In dance
the spirits lifted her
she pinched her arms as she watched
herself float.
The squirrels talked about virgins
and newlyweds.
The water wanted to know
where she would go.

Her husband was the healer.
He went in the sweatlodge,
ate the people's offering
of deer and rabbit roast.
He was given Eagle feathers
while she
received the thousand eyes of flies.

The cats arched, scratched and hissed
behind the half-ton cab.
She knew
she'd find their fingernails
in a ball of bones and fur,
the owl's feast of fat.

In the woods with ink and paper leaves
she met her lover. He flowing beneath
her feet, crackling knuckles in the wind,
gurgling near the beaver dam. They argued
about geezuz and the origin of man, spun stories
in the dance of their tongues.

***

Her husband said he was reaching
forty and wished to plant roots.
In sleep she visited fields
of wheat and straw
dancing in waves, wrapped in
clouds. The trees cradled her
passing her
back and forth,
arm to arm.

The city never sees the dawn.
A magpie scolds her return.
The water's tongue is frozen beneath
hot sewage and glacial barges.
She keeps falling down carpet stairs.
The spirits laugh in darkness
while the silence eats.

The fruitful feast of forty:
cranberries and currents
hives in high branches
thorns catching jeans, scratches
of bears at anthills, calling
loons in blueberry flats
all caught on paper leaves.
She's flown with the best of them,
free in their knowing.

The dogs are in the city
tonguing rain off her face.
Their guts wring
in her fingers, skulls howling
in the trees, moon lovers in
meadows.

The woods map her dreams
the west wind braids
strands of grey hair
to the earth in her feet.

The Eagle Squeeze

I've wandered the wilderness
running after your shadow
plucking fluffs from your belly
dragging my cord.
The eggs in your mouth
you dropped at my doorstep
babies featherless as your smile.

I'm skinned-drum,
beating stick in your hand.
My tits flat.
I throb thick,
old bloody stories sung.
Ratroot trickling
through my heart. Steam from your body
sweating into my robes
bones buckling beneath the rock.

> Yes, I snuggle deep into him
> twenty years of wind he blows in his sleep.
> Yes, I've swum and swallowed
> the slippery sweat of his pores.
> My belly drummed
> little heels against my heart.
> I've cried, cursed and laughed the
> raw babies.
> Yes, we ate off boxes,
> selling his grandfather's coins for food.
> Built our first table with planks
> the spirits lifted.
> He Sundanced,
> the dew on my cheeks won't rub away.

Your thunder drums
on my waiting belly.
Your wings span the prairie warriors dance.
Dip and bend,
    dip and bend,
dip and bend

feather fluffs,
clouds and tents open in the sun.
My outstretched palm heavy, gold
reflecting in your eye.

        Yes, many hours I spend alone,
        children hanging from my tits.
        He slumbered over formaldehyde
        pickled bodies of the dead.
        Yes, I touched the warm space beside my bed,
        he rushing out in forty below
        to patch the beaten drunk,
        hold the widow,
        and deliver the frozen baby.
        Yes, frogs mat the carpet
        beneath my feet
        and I wear the Onassis dress.
        We are spoons in sleep,
        butterflies fluttering on my neck,
        sweet whisperings, sweetgrass in the air.

The shadow dances
hanging from my neck.
I move from the rock
gathering goose eggs.
I shall weave my basket
from the hairs I pluck from
your brown arms,
spin my lovers eye's, emerald suns.
I shall fill my belly
with the spill from your beak.
I'll fold the eggs
in winter skin
cradled in sleep.
My grandmother's rump
hot and broad as your prairie wings.

Afterword – Comfortable in My Bones

In the Northern woods of Saskatchewan lies a creek; in the summer, it's a slender, lazy snail. When the spring rains come, it becomes a writhing snake creating turbulent waves, carrying everything before it. I walked the woods, following the creek, cradling paper leaves and talking stick, tobacco and sweetgrass in my hands. On many occasions, I flew over logs in front of me eager to gain my solitude, eager to unload the discoveries I held close to my heart. My favourite spot overlooked the banks where I leaned against an old log I shared with ants. There, I contemplated something I had read, something I heard on CBC, something I dreamt, a conversation I had with my children or my husband. Sometimes, these discoveries were not pretty. My journeys became a ritual where I offered tobacco and smudged with sweetgrass. Whatever travelled into my thoughts, I immediately wrote, no matter how absurd or obscure. At times, I did nothing but breathe, listen and sleep, comfortable in my bones. The landscape of the earth and my mind were both simple and complex. I bore feelings that needed song. I often suffered the rash of shame bursting through the thin layers of skin. Yet my spirit demanded the spring of clear blood. I saw no need to run. The land, the Spirit doesn't betray you. I was learning to cry with the Spirit. I was safe to tear, to lick, to strip the stories from my bones and to offer them to the universe.

When I was a child, I was taught to lift a found bone from the earth and scrape my warts, then to return it the way it was found. Many times, I watched my cousin grind bones for my grandmother, medicines she added to her bundles. I was grinding my own bones. Through the leaves and pen, the elusive became concrete. My voice rose through my scribble. On many occasions, I had watched my grandfather's long johns held by a string, flopping, waving, rolling on the edge of the culvert. We always knew when laundry day was. The foam the creek made provided the soap he didn't have. During our courting days, my husband and I would strip in the spring April heat, bask in the sun and plunge in the glacial Whiterabbit

River on Kootenay Plains. The strength of the water replenishes and destroys, the calling of the creek and my return are a natural process.

The year rolled into two, three, four: my journals accumulated. The Great Mystery entered my dreams, and I heard its voice through its creation. Squirrels shared their chatter, the wind blew its soul into my ears, and the water spoke its very ancient tongue. These stirrings were not unfamiliar since I come from a place where all creation and its gifts are naturally accepted. I went to the elders and spoke to them about my dreams and my revelations. I entered ritual once again to receive my spiritual name and to honour my journey. I had a dream many years ago that I was repairing the cabin I grew up in with paper and books. I had entered this ceremony, the stirring of my marrow, a living prayer of building and healing, feeding my soul. I read a wide range of authors, including Joseph Campbell, Carl Jung, Mary Daly, Mathew Fox, Sheila Watson, Louise Erdich, and numerous anthologies written by female and Native writers. My curiosity challenged, I covered topics around sexual morals, philosophy, religious and spiritual debates, symbols, myths and legends. I hoarded my solitude jealously, and became angry when I wasn't fulfilling these needs.

The map of oral storytelling had long been laid out for me. I often entertained my children with legends I grew up with or made up on my own through the images in classical music. Writing was a natural process. The stories inside me demanded face. They became my medicine, creating themselves in the form of poetry. These egg-bones were the voice which I have been addressing. My bare feet had felt the drum of the earth and the heartbeat of my palms. I did not fight these stories, though many times I wanted to run. I became a wolf, sniffing and searching, pawing, muzzling, examining every visible track I made or saw. I became the predator on the scent. I was the master, the slave, beholder and beheld, the voice and the song. I was the dark, the light. Like the legend of *Pāhkahkos*, my death-song grated, and when I honoured my history *Pāhkahkos* rattled her bones in the gourds of my memory. I will no longer be a binding sinew of stifling rules, but rather a sinew of wolf songs, clear as morning air.

Glossary

sihkos . . . . *weasel*
iskwew . . . . *woman*
ahcāhk . . . . *soul/spirit*
paskwāw-mostos . . . . *buffalo*
ayamihāwina . . . . *rituals, prayer*
Pāhkahkos . . . . *Flying Skeleton, mythical spirit of the Cree*
Nōhkom ātayohkān . . . . *Grandmother of the legends*
Nōhkom . . . . *my Grandmother*
ayisīniw . . . . *human being, person*
cācāmosikan . . . . *sneezing root*
hāw . . . . *now or okay*
kiskiman . . . . *sharp tail bone; literal translation: file*
asam . . . . *feed*
picikiskisīs . . . . *chickadee*
āmōmey . . . . *honey; literal translation: bee shit*
āstam . . . . *come*
mihkwāskikan . . . . *robin*
kinepīk . . . . *snake*
Nimosōm . . . . *my Grandfather*
apiscāskōc . . . . *prairie bird*
awāsisak . . . . *children*
pekīwe . . . . *come home*
Wīsahkecāhk . . . . *Cree trickster*
kīmōc . . . . *in secret*
micakisīs . . . . *little gut, penis*

Stanza (This song is sung by many Plains Cree people.)
    Waniskā . . . . *Get up*
    pe wāpan ōma . . . . *dawn arrives*
    āsay piyesīsak . . . . *already birds*
    nikamowak . . . . *sing*
    miyohtākwan . . . . *a beautiful sound*
    kitaskīnaw . . . . *of our earth, our land.*

nīcimos . . . . *girlfriend/boyfriend*
namōya māskoc . . . . *it's not so*
nitotem . . . . *my relative, could be anyone*
Nehiyawak . . . . *the Cree, the People*
e-pimisik . . . . *she lays*

Stanza

Pasikōk, pasikōk	*Get up, get up*
pehtāw, pehtāw	*listen, listen, as in hear, hear*
kisimsinow pikiskwew	*our younger sibling speaks*
akosiwak ayisiyiniwāk	*the people are sick*
piko matotsānihk ta	
pimātisīyahk	*we must go into the sweatlodge to be alive*
kīpa kīwek	*hurry home*
kākīsimotāk	*pray, implore*
iskwew atoskewin	
kimiyikonaw	*a woman delegated work to us*
kakweyāhok, kakweyāhok	*hurry, hurry*
tā kākīsimoyāhk	*let's all pray*
ahaw	*it's okay, amen*

sōniyās	*money*
mōnīyās	*white person*
Iyiniwak	*People*
Manitou	*Creator, God*
isistāwina	*rituals*
mātotsān	*sweatlodge*
kimoti	*to steal*
wēpāyōs	*wagging tail*
wanuskewin	*tranquility, to make a turn in life, a heritage site in Saskatoon*
kīwētinohk	*north, going home*
Nōhkomāk	*more than one grandmother*
Wīhtikōw	*Ice being, cannibal*
pisikwātisiw	*loose, run around*

Acknowledgements

Several of these poems have appeared in the following magazines and anthologies: *NeWest Review, Residential Schools: The Stolen Years, Vintage '92, Tratti 30* (Italy), and *Writing the Circle.* Other poems have been broadcast on CBC Radio's "Ambience," CBC Radio's "Morningside," and CBC-FM's "Arts Tonight."

The author wishes to acknowledge the Saskatchewan Arts Board for its assistance in making this book possible. Special thanks for the wonderful support and guidance provided by the Saskatchewan Writers Guild, Sage Hill Writing Experience, Coteau Books, CBC Radio, Wayne Schmalz, and Sylvia Vance, editor of *Writing the Circle.* Sincere appreciation to my mentors and Elders: Vera Martin, Campbell Papaquash, Tony and Emma Sand, Maria Campbell, Joe and Jenny Cardinal. A most special tribute to my energetic editor, Patrick Lane; my first critic, Peter Butt; and word master consultant, Ron Marken. Thank you Stan Cuthand for the Cree spelling bee and Ruth Cuthand for the powerful book cover. Thanks to Nancy Waskewitch, Martha Half, and Mom and Dad for sharing this fine and exciting journey. Sincere gratitude to David and Fran Barnes, Patti Mulford, Ruth and Frank Morin, Lorna Crozier, Nechi Staff and fellow trainees for friendship, laughter and tears. Thank you to all those many, many others whose names I've failed to mention, you've danced with me in this musical world on all its chords. Last and most important, to my delightful children Omeasoo and Usine and my husband, Peter, thank you for your love, endless support, encouragement and the journey. All my relations. Ahow. – Sky Dancer

The publisher wishes to thank Judy Bear and Mary Jane Eley of the Saskatchewan Indian Federated College for their assistance with the Cree spellings and translations.

PHOTO: DON DENTON

About the Author

LOUISE BERNICE HALFE's Cree name is Sky Dancer. She was born to Saddle Lake Reserve in Alberta in 1953. At the age of seven, she was sent away to Blue Quills Residential School in St. Paul, Alberta. She left home of her own accord when she was sixteen, breaking ties with her family and completing her studies at St. Paul's regional high school. It was at this time that she began writing a journal about her experiences.

Halfe made her debut as a poet in *Writing the Circle: Native Women of Western Canada*, the acclaimed anthology of life-writings by Native women. In 1993, she was awarded third prize in the League of Canadian Poets' national poetry contest. She has a Bachelor of Social Work from the University of Regina and certificates in addictions counselling from the Nechi Institute. Halfe lives in Saskatoon with her husband and two children.

About the Cover Artist

RUTH CUTHAND is a visual artist who currently resides in Saskatoon. She received her MFA from the University of Saskatchewan in 1992. Cuthand has exhibited her work throughout Canada; her most recent exhibition was "Location/Dislocation" at the Mendel Art Gallery in Saskatoon during the summer of 1993.